Made in the USA
Monee, IL
31 May 2025

18527959R00059